out of

WONDER WORLD

I think you come

A book of children's verse
chosen & illustrated by

JESSICA BAILEY

images
Publishing
(Malvern) Ltd

First published in South Africa 1994 by
Bailey's African Photo Archives
PO Box 37
Lanseria
1748
South Africa

This revised edition first published in Great Britain 1994 by
Images Publishing (Malvern) Ltd.
Upton upon Severn
Worcestershire

British Library Cataloguing in Publication Data

A catalogue record for this book is available
from the British Library

ISBN 1 897817 49 5

Designed and Produced by Images Publishing (Malvern) Ltd.
Printed and Bound in Great Britain.

The author wishes to point that some of the poems which appear in this anthology are extracts from longer works: *From the Bridge* by John Keats is taken from *I stood tip-toe upon a little hill; To See a World* by William Blake is taken from *Auguries of Innocence*; and *Song* by William Shakespeare is taken from *Hamlet*. Other poems not included in their entirety are: *A Boy's Song* by John Keats; *Summer Sun* by Robert Louis Stevenson; *The Passionate Shepherd to his Love* by Christopher Marlowe; *Queen Mab* by Thomas Hood; *Night* by William Blake; *The Rock-a-Bye Boat* by Mary Farrah; and *The Barefoot Boy* by John Greenleaf Whittier.

Finally, the author and the publisher wish to thank Margaret Clark for her assistance in checking proofs and sources; and The Literary Trustees of Walter de la Mare, and The Society of Authors as their representative, for permission to reproduce *Silver* by Walter de la Mare. Whilst every effort has been made to trace the copyright owners of the other poems reproduced in this book, there do remain at least two quoted for which the sources are unknown to the author and publisher. The publisher will be glad to hear from the copyright owners of these poems in order to rectify the position and make due acknowledgement in all future editions of this book.

Contents

For Frederick and Imogen
and for Jim, with love

LEISURE

What is this life if, full of care,
We have no time to stand and stare.

No time to stand beneath the boughs
And stare as long as sheep or cows.

No time to see, when woods we pass,
Where squirrels hide their nuts in grass.

No time to see, in broad daylight,
Streams full of stars like skies at night.

No time to turn at Beauty's glance,
And watch her feet, how they can dance.

No time to wait till her mouth can
Enrich that smile her eyes began.

A poor life this if, full of care,
We have no time to stand and stare.

W. H. Davies

A BOY'S SONG

Where the pools are bright and deep,
Where the grey trout lies asleep,
Up the river and over the lea,
That's the way for Billy and me.

James Hogg

FROM THE BRIDGE

How silent comes the water round that bend,
Not the minutest whisper does it send
To the o'erhanging sallows; blades of grass
Slowly across the chequered shadows pass.

John Keats

SUMMER SUN

Great is the sun, and wide he goes
Through empty heaven without repose;
And in the blue and glowing days
More thick than rain he showers his rays.

Robert Louis Stevenson

THE BAREFOOT BOY

Blessings on thee, little man,
Barefoot boy, with cheek of tan!
With thy turned-up pantaloons,
And thy merry whistled tunes;
With thy red lip, redder still
Kissed by strawberries on the hill;
With the sunshine on thy face,
Through thy torn brim's jaunty grace;
From my heart I give thee joy —
I was once a barefoot boy!

John Greenleaf Whittier

RAIN

The rain is raining all around,
It falls on field and tree;
It rains on the umbrellas here,
And on the ships at sea.

Robert Louis Stevenson

TO SEE A WORLD

To see a World in a Grain of Sand
And a Heaven in a Wild Flower,
Hold Infinity in the palm of your hand
And Eternity in an hour.

William Blake

WHERE GO THE BOATS?

Dark brown is the river,
    Golden is the sand.
It flows along for ever,
    With trees on either hand.

Green leaves a-floating,
    Castles of the foam,
Boats of mine a-boating —
    Where will all come home?

On goes the river
    And out past the mill,
Away down the valley,
    Away down the hill.

Away down the river,
    A hundred miles or more,
Other little children
    Shall bring my boats ashore.

Robert Louis Stevenson

A KITE

I often sit and wish that I
Could be a kite up in the sky,
And ride upon the breeze and go
Whichever way I chanced to blow.
Then I could look beyond the town,
And see the river winding down,
And follow all the ships that sail
Like me before the merry gale,
Until at last with them I came
To some place with a foreign name.

Frank Dempster Sherman

WHO HAS SEEN THE WIND?

Who has seen the wind?
   Neither I nor you:
But when the leaves hang trembling
   The wind is passing through.

Who has seen the wind?
   Neither you nor I:
But when the trees bow down their heads
   The wind is passing by.

Christina Rossetti

MY KINGDOM

Down by a shining water well
I found a very little dell,
   No higher than my head.
The heather and the gorse about
In summer bloom were coming out,
   Some yellow and some red.

   I called the little pool a sea;
   The little hills were big to me;
      For I am very small,
   I made a boat, I made a town,
   I searched the caverns up and down,
      And named them one and all.

   And all about was mine, I said,
   The little sparrows overhead,
      The little minnows too.
   This was the world and I was king;
   For me the bees came by to sing,
      For me the swallows flew.

I played there were no deeper seas,
Nor any wider plains than these,
   Nor other kings than me.
At last I heard my mother call
Out from the house at even-fall,
   To call me home to tea.

And I must rise and leave my dell,
And leave my dimpled water well,
   And leave my heather blooms.
Alas! And as my home I neared
How very big my nurse appeared,
How great and cool the rooms!

Robert Louis Stevenson

FLOWER FANCIES

Lily, fair Lily,
    Why are you all in white?
"Child, I was born of the pale moonlight:
Where it fell through the night
    Dank and chilly,
And touched with splendour the dreaming earth,
    There had I birth."

    Tall Sunflower,
Where got you your disk of yellow?
"From the golden sun that laughed as I leapt
To greet him king without fellow!
He passed, but his smile I kept
Through storm and through shower –
    A life-long dower."

Rose, sweet Rose,
Why is your heart so red?
   "From splendours shed
When the sky was a-flame with the sunset light;
The crimson paled, and the day was dead;
   But its lustre a rosebud knows,
     Born that night."

Flowers, you are fairies, I know:
   Have you gifts to bestow?
"Fain would we give thee thoughts as white
As the Lily; a smile still bright
As hers who is loved by the sun;
   And a heart that glows
Like the living heart of the Rose,
With love for God's creatures every one,
   Till life be done."

Anon

I MET A MAN

I met a man who asked of me,
"How many strawberries grow in the sea?"
I answered him as I thought good,
"As many herrings as grow in the wood."

Anon

THE COW

The friendly cow, all red and white,
    I love with all my heart;
She gives me cream with all her might,
    To eat with apple tart.

She wanders lowing here and there,
    And yet she cannot stray,
All in the pleasant open air,
    The pleasant light of day;

And blown by all the winds that pass
And wet with all the showers,
She walks among the meadow grass
And eats the meadow flowers.

Robert Louis Stevenson

I HAD A LITTLE NUT-TREE

I had a little nut-tree, nothing would it bear
But a silver nutmeg and a golden pear.
The King of Spain's daughter came to visit me,
And all for the sake of my little nut-tree.

Anon

RIDE A COCK-HORSE

Ride a cock-horse to Banbury Cross,
To see a fine lady ride upon a white horse.
Rings on her fingers and bells on her toes,
And she shall have music wherever she goes.

Anon

ELSIE MARLEY

Elsie Marley is grown so fine
She won't get up to feed the swine,
But lies in bed till eight or nine –
Lazy Elsie Marley!

Anon

THERE WAS AN OLD WOMAN

There was an old woman who lived in a shoe,
Who had so many children, she didn't know what to do.
She gave them some broth without any bread,
She whipped them all soundly, and sent them to bed.

Anon

PUSSY CAT, PUSSY CAT, WHERE HAVE YOU BEEN?

Pussy cat pussy cat, where have you been?
I've been to London to look at the queen.
Pussy cat pussy cat, what did you there?
I frightened a little mouse under her chair.

Little girl, little girl, where have you been?
Gathering roses to give to the queen.
Little girl, little girl, what gave she you?
She gave me a diamond as big as my shoe.

Anon

I HAD A LITTLE PONY

I had a little pony, his name was Dapple Grey;
I lent him to a lady to ride a mile away.
She whipped him, she slashed him,
    she rode him through the mire:
I would not lend my pony now,
    for all the lady's hire.

THE OWL AND THE PUSSY-CAT

The Owl and the Pussy-cat went to sea
In a beautiful pea-green boat;
They took some honey, and plenty of money
Wrapped up in a five-pound note.
The Owl looked up to the stars above,
And sang to a small guitar,
"O lovely Pussy, O Pussy, my love,
What a beautiful Pussy you are,
You are,
You are,
What a beautiful Pussy you are!"

Pussy said to the Owl, "You elegant fowl,
How charmingly sweetly you sing!
Oh! let us be married; too long have we tarried:
But what shall we do for a ring?"
They sailed away for a year and a day,
To the land where the Bong-tree grows,
And there in the wood a Piggy-wig stood,
With a ring at the end of his nose,
His nose,
His nose,
With a ring at the end of his nose.

"Dear Pig, are you willing to sell for one shilling
Your ring?" Said the Piggy, "I will."
So they took it away, and were married next day
By the turkey who lives on the hill.
They dined on mince and slices of quince,
Which they ate with a runcible spoon;
And hand in hand, on the edge of the sand,
They danced by the light of the moon,
The moon,
The moon,
They danced by the light of the moon.

Edward Lear

THE PASSIONATE SHEPHERD TO HIS LOVE

Come live with me and be my Love,
And we will all the pleasures prove
That hills and valleys, dale and field,
Or woods or steepy mountains yield.

And we will sit upon the rocks,
And see the shepherds feed their flocks
By shallow rivers, to whose falls
Melodious birds sing madrigals.

Christopher Marlowe

WHEN YOU AND I GROW UP

When you and I
Grow up – Polly –
   I mean that you and me
Shall go sailing in a big ship
   Right over all the sea.
We'll wait till we are older,
   For if we went today,
You know that we might lose ourselves,
   And never find the way.

                    Kate Greenaway

THE ROCK

By a flat rock on the shore of the sea
My dear one spoke to me. Wild thyme
Now grows by the rock
And a sprig of rosemary.

                    Anon.

SONG

Tomorrow is Saint Valentine's day,
All in the morning betime,
And I a maid at your window,
To be your Valentine.

William Shakespeare

GIBBERISH

Many a flower have I seen blossom,
　　Many a bird for me will sing.
Never heard I so sweet a singer,
　　Never saw I so fair a thing.

She is a bird, a bird that blossoms,
　　She is a flower, a flower that sings;
And I a flower when I behold her,
　　And when I hear her, I have wings.

Mary E. Coleridge

AROUND THE WORLD

In go-cart so tiny
   My sister I drew;
And I've promised to draw her
   The wide world through.

We have not yet started —
   I own it with sorrow —
Because our trip's always
   Put off till tomorrow.

Kate Greenaway

AEDH WISHES FOR THE CLOTHS OF HEAVEN

Had I the heavens' embroider'd cloths
Enwrought with golden and silver light,
The blue and the dim and the dark cloths
Of night and light and the half light,
I would spread the cloths under your feet:
But I, being poor, have only my dreams;
I have spread my dreams under your feet;
Tread softly because you tread on my dreams.

William Butler Yeats

QUEEN MAB

A little fairy comes at night,
Her eyes are blue, her hair is brown,
With silver spots upon her wings,
And from the moon she flutters down.

She has a little silver wand,
And when a good child goes to bed
She waves her wand from right to left,
And makes a circle round its head.

And then it dreams of pleasant things,
Of fountains filled with fairy fish,
And trees that bear delicious fruit,
And bow their branches at a wish:

Of arbours filled with dainty scents
From lovely flowers that never fade;
Bright flies that glitter in the sun,
And glow-worms shining in the shade:

And talking birds with gifted tongues,
For singing songs and telling tales,
And pretty dwarfs to show the way
Through fairy hills and fairy dales.

Thomas Hood

THE OLD WOMAN TOSSED UP IN A BASKET

There was an old woman tossed up in a basket
Ninety times as high as the moon.
And where she was going I couldn't but ask it,
For in her hand she carried a broom.
"Old woman, old woman, old woman!" quoth I,
"O Whither, O Whither, O Whither so high?"
"To sweep the cobwebs off the sky."
"Can I go with you?"
"Aye, Bye and Bye."

Anon

WEE WILLIE WINKIE

Wee Willie Winkie runs through the town,
Upstairs and downstairs in his nightgown.
Rapping at the window, crying through the lock,
"Are the children all in bed, for now it's eight o'clock!"

Anon

OVERHEARD ON A SALT MARSH

Nymph, nymph, what are your beads?
Green glass, goblin. Why do you stare at them?
Give them me.
                    No.'
Give them me. Give them me.
                                No.
Then I will howl all night in the reeds.
Lie in the mud and howl for them.

Goblin, why do you love them so?

They are better than stars or water,
Better than voices of winds that sing,
Better than any man's fair daughter,
Your green glass beads on a silver ring.

Hush, I stole them out of the moon.

Give me your beads, I desire them.
                                No.
I will howl in a deep lagoon
For your green glass beads, I love them so.
Give them me. Give them.
                    No.

Harold Monro

THE SECRET PLAYMATE

When I am playing underneath the tree,
I look around — and there he is with me!

Among the shadows of the boughs he stands,
And shakes the leaves at me with both his hands.

And then upon the mossy roots we lie,
And watch the leaves make pictures on the sky.

And then we swing and float from bough to bough —
And never fall? I can't remember how.

The games I play with him are always best,
And yet we cannot teach them to the rest.

For when the others come to join our play,
I look around — and he has slipped away!

They ask me if he speaks — I cannot tell,
But no one else can play with me so well.

Josephine Bacon

FROM WONDER WORLD

Out of Wonder World I think you come;
For in your eyes the wonder comes with you.
The stars are the windows of Heaven,
And sometimes I think you peep through.
Oh, little girl, tell us do the Flowers
Tell you secrets when they find you all alone?
Or the Birds and Butterflies whisper
Of things to us unknown?

Kate Greenaway

A FAREWELL

My fairest child, I have no song to give you;
    No lark could pipe to skies so dull and grey;
Yet, ere we part, one lesson I can leave you
    For every day.

Be good, sweet maid, and let who will be clever;
    Do noble things, not dream them, all day long
And so make life, death, and that vast forever
    One grand, sweet song.

Charles Kingsley

NIGHT

The sun descending in the west,
The evening star does shine;
The birds are silent in their nest,
And I must seek for mine.
The moon, like a flower,
In heaven's high bower,
With silent delight
Sits and smiles on the night.

William Blake

SILVER

Slowly, silently, now the moon
Walks the night in her silver shoon;
This way, and that, she peers, and sees
Silver fruit upon silver trees;
One by one the casements catch
Her beams beneath the silvery thatch;
Couched in his kennel, like a log,
With paws of silver sleeps the dog;
From their shadowy cote the white breasts peep
Of doves in a silver-feathered sleep;
A harvest mouse goes scampering by,
With silver claws, and silver eye;
And moveless fish in the water gleam,
By silver reeds in a silver stream.

Walter de la Mare

THE LAND OF NOD

From breakfast on all through the day
At home among my friends I stay;
But every night I go abroad
Afar into the Land of Nod.

All by myself I have to go,
With none to tell me what to do –
All alone beside the streams
And up the mountainsides of dreams.

Try as I like to find the way,
I never can get back by day,
Nor can remember plain and clear
The curious music that I hear.

Robert Louis Stevenson

THE ROCK-A-BY BOAT

When the lamps are lit in the silver skies
   And mother says, "Time for bed,"
When the bairnies close their drooping eyes,
   And the last "good night" is said,
Away on a wonderful voyage they float
   Far over the ocean deep,
From the Land of Nod in the Rock-a-By Boat
   To the magic City of Sleep.

Mary Farrah

MINNIE AND WINNIE

Minnie and Winnie
    Slept in a shell.
Sleep, little ladies!
    And they slept well.

Pink was the shell within,
    Silver without;
Sounds of the great sea
    Wandered about.

Sleep, little ladies!
    Wake not soon!
Echo on echo
    Dies to the moon.

Two bright stars
    Peeped into the shell.
"What are they dreaming of?
    Who can tell?"

Started a green linnet
    Out of the croft;
Wake, little ladies!
    The sun is aloft.

Alfred, Lord Tennyson

WYNKEN, BLYNKEN AND NOD

Wynken, Blynken, and Nod one night
   Sailed off in a wooden shoe —
Sailed on a river of crystal light,
   Into a sea of dew.
"Where are you going, and what do you wish?"
   The old moon asked the three.
"We have come to fish for the herring fish
   That live in this beautiful sea;
   Nets of silver and gold have we!"
     Said Wynken,
     Blynken,
     And Nod.

The old moon laughed and sang a song,
   As they rocked in the wooden shoe,
And the wind that sped them all night long
   Ruffled the waves of dew.
The little stars were the herring fish
   That lived in that beautiful sea —
"Now cast your nets wherever you wish —
   Never afeared are we;"
   So cried the stars to the fishermen three:
     Wynken,
     Blynken,
     And Nod.

Wynken and Blynken are two little eyes,
    And Nod is a little head,
And the wooden shoe that sailed the skies
    Is a wee one's trundle-bed.
So shut your eyes while mother sings
    Of wonderful sights that be,
And you shall see the beautiful things
    As you rock in the misty sea,
    Where the old shoe rocked the fishermen three:
        Wynken,
        Blynken,
        And Nod.

All night long their nets they threw
    To the stars in the twinkling foam —
Then down from the skies came the wooden shoe,
    Bringing the fishermen home;
'Twas all so pretty a sail it seemed
    As if it could not be,
And some folks thought 'twas a dream they'd dreamed
    Of sailing that beautiful sea —
    But I shall name you the fishermen three:
        Wynken,
        Blynken,
        And Nod.

Eugene Field